UP AND DOWN THE RIVER

HARPER & ROW, PUBLISHERS
New York   Hagerstown   San Francisco   London

UP AND DOWN THE RIVER

BOAT POEMS

by CLAUDIA LEWIS

pictures by BRUCE DEGEN

To my niece,
Marie Lewis Matthews,
with love

Up and Down the River

Text copyright © 1979 by Claudia Lewis
Illustrations copyright © 1979 by Bruce Degen
For information address
Harper & Row, Publishers, Inc., 10 East 53rd Street,
New York, N.Y. 10022. Published simultaneously in
Canada by Fitzhenry & Whiteside Limited, Toronto.

First Edition

Library of Congress Cataloging in Publication Data
Lewis, Claudia Louise, date
    Up and down the river.

    SUMMARY: Thirteen poems that characterize
the different kinds of boats that sail down a
busy river.
    1. Boats and boating—Juvenile poetry.
[1. Boats and boating—Poetry.   2. American
poetry]   I. Degen, Bruce.   II. Title.
PZ8.3.L585Up   811'.5'4   78-22494
ISBN 0-06-023812-7
ISBN 0-06-023813-5 lib. bdg.

Off to Work in the Morning

A duck boat,
neck up, head up,
flat back,
paddle-foot, paddle-foot,
up, up the river.

Fairy-Tale Morning

On the river,
sky-blue,
whitecaps whipping up, splashing
white sea gulls dipping
        over the dotted water
like bits of foam
flicked up, flashing—

And on this bright bird-sea
a small white boat
with a white blown sail
white as a gull—
magical!

(Bearing a prince,
a swan,
the seventh one?

Bearing home
the brother and sister
lost so long?)

Wave tips splashing
foam birds flashing
out of the windy blue,
flicking up magic
old as old, and gone,
yet still—
        sparkling new.

The Coast Guard Cutter

Above
    white as a flying gull
Below
    black licorice
    (looks eatable!)
Up front
    one stripe, painted red
Watch her —
    smashing up billows
    as she speeds ahead!

Markings

Whizzing by,
a small boat
with a motor
cutting its mark,
a long *V*,
on the water—
A *V* that flows
and slowly grows
as wide as the river—

Wide and long—
Yet I know there are *V*s
flowing
   growing
      greater
         than these—

those airy markings
no one sees.

Waiting

The long river and the low cliff border lie
still and grey under
the winter sky—
the land snow-streaked.

Waiting
No boats pass; no birds fly—

> Flash!
> Red!
> a tug
> bounding by
> red, with a barge
> !Bright color!
> on the grey water
> (Hello, captain!)

Waiting.

Queens of the River

STAR NADINE, GOLDEN SPEAR, GYPSUM KING
floating along
majestically—

CHROMALLOY, MANISTEE
loaded with crates,
with oil,
ships of industry—

NORTHERN EAGLE OF MONROVIA, DAPHNE
colors flat, plain,
black and white,
faded green,

but on the bows the beautiful names—

NEPCO COURAGEOUS, GOLDEN ENDEAVOR
to let the world know
that only they are
            kings of the sea
            queens of the river.

Out for a Ride

A little puff boat,
white as a marshmallow,
whiffing down the river.

At Work, on the River

The orange sun
       burned a fiery scorch on the water
              screaming-blinding-bright
       shook flame into the sky-mist,
       struck at the windowpanes
       and sifted airy orange light
              into white rooms—

       sank, then, smouldering,
              a round red ball
       rippling up the clouds with scarlet.

              Down below on the river
              a tug-and-barge
              chugged slowly south,
                     at work.

October Haze

Under the smoke-haze
the sunset sky is
like a shell, pink
and the water, pale;
a white sail moves south
through the delicate
color

and I breathe
delicately
and am drawn
in a soft way
into the scene—

Night Magic

A barge is moving
down the still river,
a great dark turtle
pushing along
leaving rippling footprints.

And now the deep reflections of the shore lights—
slender candles in the water—
quiver and curve,
quiver and curve in the ripples
gently,
then turning, turning
till suddenly—
      barber's poles!
      tremulous,
      soft with yellow light,
twisting and twinkling
where tall candles stood before
in sunken dim cathedrals.

—Old turtle's doing.
There he goes
plodding on
toward home
kicking up ripples
behind him.

Frightening!

Here it comes!
    huge hulk
    in the darkness
    the long freighter
    blacker than the water
    silent as a ghostship
    stealing by
    slowly
    down the dark river.

Reflections:
The Sightseeing Boat After Dark

Underwater circus act!
    Little lighted fishes
    trout-shaped
    standing on their tail fins
    nibbling nibbling gentle nibbles
    to keep the boat
    afloat—

Jewels Floating By

The little tugboats
circled with lights—
kings' crowns
cast upon the water.

To my friend Sam
who introduced me to the river

—BD